Victim to Victory
There is Healing in the Release:
From Diagnosis to Mission

Joanne Saulsberry

ISBN:
ISBN-13:

This is a work of creative nonfiction based on actual events. They are presented based on the memory of the author, Joann Saulsberry. All persons mentioned have provided a written consent and release form giving the author permission and waiving rights to any royalties and liability.

DEDICATION

For Gerald Saulsberry
My Soulmate for Life
A man I've always admired…
The man that's been by my side through it all.
The best husband a girl could ask for.

CONTENTS

	Acknowledgments	i
1	Come Take This Journey With Me	1
2	Victim in Adulthood	14
3	Victory in Adulthood	32
4	Transition to Victory	39
5	Set Back to be Set Up	45
6	Another Storm	59
7	Lessons Learned	66
	Everyday Meditation Instructions	68
	Healing Scriptures	69

As you take this journey with me I pray its healing and deliverance in these pages. It has been a journey but I wouldn't take nothing for my journey. You see my glory now read my story to match this glory.

I give all Glory to God.

ACKNOWLEDGMENTS

First I'd like to thank God for His love and never giving up on me, even when I wanted to give up. Without God nothing is possible and I'm forever thankful and grateful.

To my soul mate for life: my husband, my very best friend, Gerald Saulsberry. You are truly the wind beneath my wings. I love you with every fiber of my soul. Your support and love has remained unconditional since the very beginning and I thank God every single day of my life.

I also want to thank my daughters Jamillia and Christy Westmoreland for their unconditional love and support. I love both of you so much. And to my two heartbeats my grandchildren Christianna Marie and Christian LaMarr. You both are Grannie's reason to fight.

To my support team: my mother Lena Westmoreland, my sisters Linda Westmoreland and Doris Sowah, My best friends Detrice Stacey Washington, Connie Curry, Shalonda Kuhn, the late Betty Childress (who I miss dearly. This book is for you). Terri Jackson, Mildred Richard Edwards, and Joseph Mitchell (miss you so much). You all have never changed with me since day one.

I also want to thank my former coworkers: Angel Martin, Norman Hill and Dr. Kenneth Grosshart; and my own Dr. Imad Omer. You all have made this whole ordeal much easier. Thanks for your unwavering support.

Much love to my spiritual supporters: my pastor, Pastor Ruby Holland, Accomplishing Word Ministry; and Pastor Lat-Doir and Lady Kimberly Glasper for your prayers, guidance and instructions.

Last but not least my author friends: LaKesha Ford-Calhoun and Anna Black; as well as my favorite author Kimberla Lawson Roby for the encouragement to put my life on these pages. Finally, my right hand lady that help make all this possible Preamiller McKinney. Your instruction and guidance has made this process so easy and rewarding. Thank you, thank you, thank you!

Come Take This Journey with Me

God has always been a constant presence in my life. Have I always been obedient? No, but I always knew there was something special about the name of Jesus early.

Since childhood, I've wanted the approval and acceptance of my mother. There was no doubt she loved me, but I never had the mother/daughter bond I'd always wanted.

I was always active in school, from head start to high school, and would participate in everything. When I was in high school my mother was a seamstress and made all my dresses for proms, pageants and other functions in school. She even made the majorette uniforms because I was a member of the band.

Now, as an adult, I realize why my mother couldn't do all the extra things I wanted to do with her. It was because she was working, trying to make ends meet, after becoming a single parent when I was ten. There was no doubt she loved me. We just didn't have the bond I had with my father.

I knew my father loved me unconditionally. (I was a daddy's girl). But I longed for the relationship other girls had with their mothers. I wanted us to do things like go to the movies together or attend functions specifically for mothers and daughters or just hang out. I don't blame my mother. Her behavior is a result of the way she was raised by her mother. My grandmother never did things with my mother as a child. I would often hear my mother say that her father was more interested in her doing the things she loved to do such as becoming a hair dresser. Of all my mother's siblings, she was the responsible one. She spent most of her time maintaining the house and helping her other siblings. Also my grandmother was not the most affectionate person and wasn't the type to say "I love you." Her mother also didn't have the means to do extra things with them. I didn't understand all this until I became an adult, living on my own and until I became a mother. She kept me clothed, fed and sheltered. That was how she showed me love.

After the divorce, when my father was no longer in the house for me, I felt like my siblings were closer to my mother than I was and I began to resent them and their relationships with her. In turn, they became envious of the relationship I had with my father. Can we say "vicious cycle?"

My father was a constant presence in my childhood even when he and my mother divorced and my dad moved to Shaw, Mississippi. During the summer months after my parents got divorced, I would go to Shaw to stay with my dad. I was so excited that I would have my clothes packed a month early. Every Friday I would get off the bus, so excited to see my daddy's red truck waiting for me. Every summer from age ten to high school, I stayed in Shaw. I looked forward to summers because I would go and spend the whole summer with him. I was a daddy's girl and my daddy spoiled me with breakfast in bed and gave me everything I wanted. He is responsible for me loving the rodeo and chewing gum. Every day he would buy me a pack of Juicy Fruit. Even when he was living with us he would give me gum every night.

When I was eight years old, we started going to the rodeo every year at Parchman State Prison. My daddy would dress me as a cowgirl: hat, boots, plaid shirt, a bandanna and jeans. My husband has since taken my daddy's place in taking me to the rodeo. I love the rodeo and horses because it was such a positive experience from my childhood. I have so many other fun memories with my father and I miss him so much.

Because I didn't get the attention I wanted from my mother, I sought out the attention from older women in the church. When I started going to Greater Community Temple (GCT) Church, the first person I encountered was a woman named Sister Betty Childress. She was the sweetest person ever. She took me under her wings as her daughter. I was broken from life: a divorce, going back to the single life after being married seven years, and having two teenage daughters to raise alone. We would go to prayer meetings together, fellowships at another member's house, and do other activities at church. We talked on the phone every other day.

I remember a time before she passed: I called her because I was a newlywed struggling in my marriage. She told me to come over to her house. When I arrived, I fell crying in her arms. She sat on the couch with me and I laid my head in her lap and she prayed for me and talked to me until I felt better. She was a Godsend and she is truly missed.

At the age of ten when my parents divorced I became overwhelmed with grief.   When I got old enough to date, at seventeen, my first boyfriend was twenty-eight, ten years my senior. I followed that trend into my adult life, always dating men significantly older than me. My first husband was thirteen years older and my current husband is ten years older than me.

I sought out older men to fill the void and love I was missing from my father not being in the house after my parents' divorce. When my father was in the home we did a lot of things together. But when he left and moved to Shaw, the only time I got to see him and spend time with him was during the summer, although sometimes during the week, he would meet me after school.

When I began dating the twenty-eight-year-old man, I thought I was in love with him. He gave me all the love I was missing from my father. Of course my mother didn't approve of the relationship which made me want it more, drawing me closer to him. When she forbade me to see him

I thought my life had ended. In fact, at that point I tried to commit suicide. After my mother told me I couldn't see the guy anymore, I didn't want to live.

I thought to myself, "First my father, now my boyfriend is leaving, Why?"

I was convinced my life was over, so I wrote my family a note explaining how I felt incomplete and how I thought no one loved me. I took three bottles of prescription medicine, then laid down to die. When my mother came home and found me, I was told I was drifting in and out of consciousness and foaming at the mouth. I didn't remember too much else after that. When I woke up the doctor told me that I was minutes away from death when I was brought in. I had convinced myself that this man gave me all I was missing from my father not being around. I just didn't know that I was seeking the wrong father.

So Jacob called the place Peniel, saying, "It is because I saw God face to face, and yet my life was spared. -Genesis 32:30 NIV

For most of my teenage years, I was very promiscuous and it even spilled over into adulthood as I looked for love in all the wrong places. The void I was trying to fill could not be satisfied by men, sex, prescription pain pills, or anything else.

Reflections

Describe a time in your life when you felt empty.

____

____

____

What did you do to fill that void?

____

____

____

Was there ever a time you felt envious or jealous of the relationship between your parents or siblings? If so, how did you handle it?

____

____

____

Make Jesus the Lord of your life, reverence Him by closing all doors to the enemy, giving God first place. Malachi 4:2-3

Victim of Adulthood

I moved to Chicago with one baby out of wedlock and a lot of hurt, but living in Chicago with my daughter was a great experience. It was my first time leaving home and being in a big city. Life was great until the winter came. That the cold, bone-chilling weather was unacceptable and I didn't make it through, moving back to Mississippi before Spring. I didn't know I was pregnant with my second child when I moved back. When I found out "devastated" was an understatement . I already had one baby out of wedlock, now I was about to have baby number two with a different father. My second child's father hung around for a while, but I was still unsatisfied with my life. He was there; yet I still felt alone and empty. I decided to uproot and move again to try to find a better life for us. I was a struggling single parent, living in poverty with two small children, and little to no income. I figured moving would provide better opportunities socially and financially for me and my daughters.

I and my two small children left Moorhead, Mississippi in 1990 with the clothes we had on and a one-way ticket to Atlanta, Georgia. I was still trying to find love and fill a void. My two children and I moved with my sister July of that same year. Running from a horrific past, little did I know that "me followed me." The reason my horrific past always followed me—I later realized—was because I didn't have a relationship with God. I knew of Him because I had been faithfully going to church as far back as I can remember, but I didn't have a personal relationship with God. Oh, how that made a difference. Moving to Atlanta to seek a better life for me and my girls was a big mistake. I could not image the troubles I would encounter while there.

I was always connected to a church wherever I lived, and being in Atlanta was no different. Here again my church family did more for me and my girls than my own family. I got a job and moved out on my own. Was it a struggle? Oh, yes! I did things I am not very proud of to make ends meet. I got a roommate because I needed someone to watch my children while I worked late nights. After I put my girls to bed, I went out and made extra money by stripping and performing at private parties. The money was excellent and my children and I wanted for nothing. Then my roommate moved out and I was back to square one.

Next, my baby girl's father decided that he wanted to come to Atlanta to be with his family. That didn't last long. He moved in then moved out and again it was me and my girls struggling. At the time my younger daughter's father was living with us, his brother came to stay for a while. When I was at work, he inappropriately touched my oldest daughter who was only eight years old at the time. I didn't find out until ten years later.

But it got worse. While working at a department store, I began taking clothes and money from the store. It seemed easy at first but I became greedy and got caught. The morning I was caught I went to work and everyone from top management was there. I arrived, clocked in and shortly after, they called me to the back of the store. They began questioning me and showing me receipts of items I had taken. They even told me they had a tape of me taking money. I confessed and the next thing I knew DeKalb County's finest was coming through the door with handcuffs.

I went to jail on a Friday, not knowing I would have to stay until Monday to go before the judge. Let me walk you through the Paul and Silas experience (Acts 16:25-34): Booking and checking was the most degrading thing I've ever experienced. They took me in a room and I had to remove everything I was wearing… I mean EVERYTHING! The only thing that saved me from taking off my underwear was a pantiliner because they thought my menstrual cycle was on. THANK YOU JESUS! Then they gave me an orange jumpsuit, white socks, and black slippers—my attire for the weekend. Next they handcuffed my arms and feet and took me through two locked doors to a cell about the size of a bathroom. The cell consisted of a toilet at the head of the bed, a sink in the corner, an iron bunk with a mattress as thin as a child's school mat, a sheet, an army blanket, and no pillow. The correction officer gave me one roll of tissue before closing that iron door.

My world came crumbling down. I never cried so much in my entire life. The next morning at 4 a.m. the guard hit the lock for the inmates to come out their cells. We were allowed to eat breakfast but it looked like slop, needless to say I ATE NOTHING. We also were allowed to shower after breakfast, but I didn't bathe, eat, or drink for three days. The showers were open and all the other inmates could see you showering and I couldn't bring myself to be so exposed.

I cried the whole three days; so much so that the other inmates felt sorry for me and tried to comfort me. They were letting me know everything was going to be alright and telling their stories about how many times they had been in and out of jail. Some were in there for murder, rape, drugs, theft and a lot of them were repeat offenders. The authorities considered putting me in isolation because they thought I was suicidal. That's the only thing that stopped me from crying. I didn't want to be separated from everyone else.

When we came out for breakfast we would stay out for four hours and then return to our cells. When we came out for lunch, we'd also stay out a few hours. The last outing for the evening was dinner and then we were put back in the cell until the next morning. I prayed and cried and cried and prayed for three days. Monday came and I went before the judge at ten o'clock in the morning. The guards came to get all prisoners due for court that day at seven. They chained us together at the arm and put chains on our feet and led us through an underground tunnel to the courthouse. While we were walking over, the other inmates said we were going to have the worst judge in DeKalb County.

I said to myself, "OH GOD!" I begged for God to show me favor in the eyes of the judge. I was number seven and GOD TRULY SHOWED ME FAVOR…the judge let me go on probation and restitution because I had no prior record. That was the worst three days if my life. Oh God can we say FREEDOM! NEVER TO RETURN TO THAT PLACE AGAIN! That is where my transformation began.

After I got out of jail I felt so empty, like a hole was in my heart. I was still going to church and bible study faithfully but I still felt empty. Something was missing until one day I went to the altar at Redan Baptist Church and received salvation. It felt like instantly the void was filled. That Sunday the pastor preached a powerful message entitled, "You Can Live Through This." It was like a light bulb went off in my head to let me know what I was missing. Jesus was the only one who could fill that void. I went to the altar with hands raised in total surrender and received salvation and the next Sunday I was baptized. I thought I would have immediate peace, but the devil was still on his job.

The thief comes only to steal, kill, and destroy

-John 10:10

* * *

My first husband was my best friend's brother. He was also a minister so I became a minister's wife. We met after I had gone home for a classmate's funeral. Stacey, my friend, met me in Memphis at the airport to drive me to Mississippi to attend the funeral. She introduced me to her brother whom I had never met. We had been friends since kindergarten, but I didn't know her brother. He had recently left the service and she thought we would make a good connection and we did; or so I thought!

After the funeral I rode back to Memphis with him because I was supposed to catch a flight to Atlanta the next day. He talked me into staying an extra day and paid for the later flight. There wasn't much dating because by Christmas of the same year, I and my two daughters were moving back to Memphis to be with him.

I had no intention of moving, but this man showed me

his nice house, the fancy cars and the abundance of money. The enemy heard me and gave me everything I thought I needed. I saw what I thought was a way of escape so I "prayed" and moved. I didn't wait on an answer from God, which was another big mistake. I thought I was in love, but I wasn't. I moved to Memphis and got married June 1997. I didn't know at the time that my soon-to-be husband was still married. Three months before our wedding, he divorced his third wife. I was wife number four. Now that I look back I realized that you can beg God for something and he will allow it to happen; not as a blessing but to teach you a lesson. That marriage was a lesson for me.

After four years into the marriage all hell broke loose. I endured mental, physical, and emotional abuse and began to see the marriage as something that was never supposed to happen. I prayed and prayed to get out until God spoke to me plain as day, **"You have to stay until I am ready to release you."**

I was miserable. My children were miserable. The only peace we got was when my husband, who was a truck driver, was on the road. He would leave on Thursday and return on Sunday. The saying, "the Lord won't put more on you than you can bear" is true. I had had enough by the fifth year of marriage, and I believe God started showing me signs that He was getting ready to release me from the marriage. I told my husband there were three ways he could make me leave: physically or emotionally abusc my girls; physically fight me, or cheat on me. All three of these things happened.

It started with my husband beating my daughters. I'm not talking about whipping as discipline but beating. Next he started abusing me. He never hit me with his hands but used words and sex. I know some people may wonder how can sexual abuse and rape happen in a marriage. It is possible. If you don't consent to being sexual with your mate and they physically force you, THAT'S RAPE. On numerous occasions it happened to me, especially near the end of the marriage.

Finally, he started cheating and that was the last straw. I found condoms everywhere: in his bags, our car, and his truck. People would call our home and hang up when I answered. I assumed it was the women he had been with. One morning, at about three o'clock, God woke me up and instructed me to go to my husband's computer. Every waking moment he was on the computer

I turned it on and said. "God, I don't know his

password." God literally guided my hands to enter the password and there it was: pornography and chat messages with different women—all the evidence I needed to prove his unfaithfulness.

I printed it, sat in disbelief, and asked, "God, what next?"

He instructed me not to say a word about what I found. "Okay, God I trust you," was my answer.

As I got up to go back to bed, I walked past the sofa where his clothes were and knocked his shirt to the floor. It landed at my feet and paper fell out the pocket. I picked it up and there were pictures of women he had been cheating with and letters where he told them he wasn't married but that I was his live in girlfriend. I made copies of everything and waited on instructions from God. That was the hardest wait of my life because I had to wait in silence and act as if I knew nothing.

My next instruction was to start packing. I left out a month's worth of clothes for me and my children. My husband asked my children why I was packing everything up. They told him I was putting away summer things.

I had everything packed seven months before I left. One day at work, I asked my co-worker if she knew of any places for rent. Another co-worker stated that knew a guy who had condos he was looking to rent. She put me in contact him and he allowed me to move into the condo with no credit check, no money down, and even sent the key to work by my co-worker. This was the beginning of my release from hell.

I made arrangements at work to take off on a Thursday when I knew my husband would be out of town on his truck route. The day he was scheduled to go, the trucking company decided to cancel his load. He went to work that Wednesday night and was on his way home to be off the entire weekend (the days I planned to move). Wow! That meant I had less than twenty-four hours to pack and move. I called everyone who agreed to help me move to let them know we had only that Wednesday night to get me and my daughters out and they did not hesitate to come. What was supposed to take three days took only two hours. After that, another dilemma occurred: I had my husband's car and he had mine. I kept his car for a week before I returned it to him in exchange for my car. The transition was smooth. He said nothing to me and I said nothing to him. We were separated for about six months before the divorce was final.

When I got the divorce papers in the mail, it was bittersweet. I felt like all the life had been sucked out of me before I quickly recovered and moved on with my life. Was it easy? NO IT WASN'T. But the peace I and my girls had in our one-bedroom condo was immeasurable.

Reflections

Have you ever asked God for something you thought you wanted and later realized it's not what you needed? How did you handle the situation?

____

____

____

Have you ever removed yourself from a situation and allowed things to just happen?

____

____

____

Do you feel God made you stay in a situation to teach you a lesson? Did you graduate out of that situation?

____

____

____

"You are an Overcomer Through Jesus Christ!"

-1 John 4:4

Victory in Adulthood

After my divorce was final in October 2002, I was released from a life of bondage. I joined Greater Community Temple COGIC in Memphis, Tennessee in 2001. It was the best decision I ever made. That's where my true relationship began with God. During the Women's Conference 2000, I received the Holy Ghost with the evidence of speaking in tongues. My life truly changed for the better.

While I was attending, I met Lat-Doir and Kimberly Glasper and they were God sent. They helped me work through the process of overcoming feeling empty. They helped me with my girls by buying school clothes and whatever else they needed. They prayed for me and loved me back to life. I felt like I was made whole again. The Glaspers were there for me every step of the way, and for that I am eternally grateful.

I got into ministry and got busy working and serving in the church. Life was good! But of course you know the devil was still lurking in the wings.

After moving on with my life, being on my own with my daughters and my new place, I found myself struggling again: single parent with not much income and two girls in school. It was very hard to adjust to single life, especially living saved and holy as a single lady. But thanks to God, I made it and remained celibate for five years, until I decided to date again. My first relationship after my divorce and years of singleness was with an alcoholic and drug addict. The relationship after was with a name who was controlling and very possessive. It ended as quickly as it started. The man I was dating was controlling and very possessive.

I had a rule in dating: if nothing came out of the relationship after six months, I would let it go and move on. I experienced this twice before I met who I thought was the epitome of what I prayed for—not just spiritually but physically—in a man. He was tall, slim, brown skinned and also a man of the cloth. Thinking back, I realized that he was a wolf in sheep's clothing. He walked, looked, and talked the part: everything I thought I wanted in a man. I later found out that he was a functioning drug addict. I had no idea. We had moved in together and he even joined my church.

One day after seven months of dating, he came to my job, took my car, and left for two weeks. That was the hardest two weeks of my life. Throughout the whole process, only a few people knew what I was dealing with. I still found a way to get to work and anywhere else I needed to go. I never stopped praising and worshipping God in the midst of this turmoil. At the end of the two weeks, on a Sunday, I was at church when an officer came and took me home.

When I arrived, my boyfriend was taking a shower as if the last two never happened. I was in total disbelief. That tall, dark and handsome man looked like a zombie: dark lips, blood shot eyes and awful looking skin. He had lost so much weight and both arms were bruised with needle marks. I was so distraught by his presence, that I screamed and cried and made him get all of his things and leave. I didn't care where he went, I just wanted him out of my house. My car was ruined and I had to get it fixed.

My mother felt sorry for him and later she drove him back to Rosedale, Mississippi to his sister's house. The only reason I accompanied my mother is she didn't want to go alone. After we separated, I discovered that I was pregnant even though my tubes were tied. There was an issue with the pregnancy so had a miscarriage. Needless to say, the end of that pregnancy was the end to my ties to that counterfeit. Life went on and I never heard from or saw him again.

After that, I decided I was done with dating. I poured myself into my relationship with God, my children, myself and ministry. I got busy working and serving God and life as I knew it was coming back around. Was it easy? Not by a long shot. But with the help of God, my daughters, and my church family I made it through the worst season of my life.

On to the next chapter…

Reflections

What are some of your "deal breakers" when dating?

____

____

____

Have you ever met someone and thought he/she was the one, then you found out that was not true?

____

____

____

How do you feel about being single and how do you handle singleness?

____

____

____

Use authority and resist fear!

Transition to Victory

After the last counterfeit, I promised God it was just Him and me until my king found me. In February 2008, shortly after I made that vow to God, he allowed me to meet the man I would eventually marry. I was at work, speaking to my manager, Livia Saulsberry, who was on the phone with her church member Sheba Evans. Sheba was telling Livia she had someone she wanted her to meet and I was still standing there. The conversation continued between Livia and Sheba, she told Livia the guy she wanted her to meet was Gerald Saulsberry. Livia and the gentlemen on the other line realized that they were cousins.

I was still standing at Livia's desk when she said, "Wait I have someone at my desk I want to introduce you to." I gave Livia permission to give him my information without hesitation because it just felt right. I sent him a picture of me and he sent me ALL his contact information. That was February 29th and he called the same day. We talked for hours. The next day I had a wedding to attend so we couldn't meet. We made arrangements to meet in person the following Monday. He came to pick me up and took me to dinner at Outback Steakhouse. We were having dinner and great conversation so much so that everyone had left the restaurant and the staff started putting the chairs on the table and the servers were sitting around looking at us and waiting for us to leave. No one came over and said anything, but all of a sudden the lights got dim and we got the point that it was time to go.

One rainy night after we had been dating for about a month, we had the conversation about dating, relationships and what we wanted.

I asked, "How long would you date before you ask a lady to marry you?"

He replied, "A year or two."

"Well it was nice knowing you and having dinner with you," I commented.

Before I got out of the truck, he asked me the same question.

"Six months no more than seven months." I wanted to put something on his mind. I explained my reason for the timeframe: we were both adults and we have been through enough to know what we want. I told him I was dating with a purpose and that purpose was to be married and he agreed.

After three months of going out every night since that first date, we realized we had been going to the same church. He came to Bible Study at GCT on Tuesday nights and would go to other different churches for Sunday service.

He told me how he would watch me but he was afraid to approach me. He even told me where I sat on Tuesday nights at Bible Study, although I never remember seeing him at all. I took that as God hiding me until I was ready and it was time for us to meet.

During a phone call on March 3, 2008 he asked me to marry him.

I asked, "Are you serious?"

"Yes very serious," he answered.

I said yes! We made our engagement official July 2008.

We were by a tree on a hill where Gerald said he would often pray for a wife. We moved in together shortly after that. I know it wasn't the Godly thing to do, but we did.

Reflections

Have you ever gotten to a point where you said, "God I surrender to you totally?" If so, what brought you to that point?

____

____

____

Have you ever done something without really thinking and it just felt right? How did you handle it?

____

____

____

How long do you think the dating process should be leading to engagement/marriage? Why?

____

____

____

My son, attend to my words; incline thine ear unto my sayings. Let them not depart from thine eyes; keep them in the midst of thine heart. For they are life unto those that find them, and health to all their flesh. Proverbs 4:20-22

Set Back To Be Set Up

The loss of power or dignity oftentimes accompanies hospital life. Sometimes it feels as if you are stripped of your identity, reduced to a medical chart in a hospital gown that leaves nothing to the imagination; a body that any stranger can touch, probe, and prod. Interns may arrive when you are lying half naked, there to study your body as if it were a textbook. But through all of that, I kept my dignity, pride, and faith in God.

There are two ways of being a patient. You can be meek and docile or fierce and bold. Like most, I began the first way but as I began to pray, I took on the second form thanks to God and the great support team He blessed me with.

* * *

On January 16, 2011 while I was at church, Pastor Lat-

Doir Glasper did an alter call and I went up for prayer. He laid his hands on me and said, "This sickness is not unto death. You shall live and not die."

Prior to that, I had been going to a lot of doctors—primary physician, cardiologist, all kinds of specialists—and spent a lot of money. My body felt like it was shutting down and I was in constant pain. My whole body ached, including my joints and muscles. I had a constant fever, chills, and flu-like symptoms. I even went to West Clinic to have a bone marrow test done for Leukemia and Lupus.

The last doctor I went to was Dr. David Boatright who was a rheumatologist. He was the one who called me that dreadful Monday morning, January 17th, regarding the blood work I had done. He asked if I wanted to come in to the office or receive the results over the phone. I assured him it was okay to tell me. I was informed that I had tested positive for HIV/AIDS.

After hearing the results, it felt like all the life had been sucked out of me. Everything after that was a blur. I remember screaming, trying to release the fear and pressure I felt was building inside me. After a while, it felt like an angel sat on my shoulder and reminded me of what Pastor Glasper spoke to me just twenty-four hours earlier: **You**

shall live and not die. This sickness is not unto death.
I calmed down a little then my supervisor, Livia, came to my desk and began praying for me. I was an emotional wreck and she asked me what I wanted to do. We left work and she took me to my church where Pastor Glasper met me and prayed with me and for me. I calmed down a little more, until I remembered I was newly married; a bride for only two years and three months. Fear kicked in again at the thought of telling my husband the terrible news. I was afraid he would leave me and I would have to face this alone. Pastor Glasper and I went to my mother's house. While on the way I called my husband, my children, and Pastor Glasper and told them to meet us there.

I broke the news to everyone at once. BIG MISTAKE! Everyone thought I contracted the disease from my husband. Hindsight, I should have confided in my husband alone before telling anyone else. He was my covering and I should have let him decide if we wanted to share my news. Unfortunately, I acted out of fear of the unknown. Everyone in the room was very emotional. My husband left because he didn't know how to process the information. He figured everyone would blame him.

It seems like after I got that diagnosis my health went

down fast. I was very, very ill almost near death. I was referred to an infectious disease doctor at the hospital. It was the same doctor who treated me for viral meningitis years ago. I was in and out of the hospital for six months and was on extensive antibiotics to get rid of the many infections. I had AIDS! I had twenty-three billion copies of HIV antibodies in my system, and had lost over eighty pounds. I was near death. I would be at work and doctors would call me and tell me I needed to go straight to the hospital. That happened several times within the six months.

I would stay in the hospital two weeks at a time. My body was like a pin cushion. I remember during one hospital stay they had to get tubes of blood every four hours. I was on so many antibiotics that it was evident in my urine (sorry a little graphic). BUT GOD! After numerous hospital stays and countless medicines in July 2011, the virus and infection was finally under control and I was able to start the anti-viral medication to treat the HIV. I thank God for great doctors, great medicine, and the ability to obtain it. When the odds were stacked against me God came through. Before then I was going to the West Clinic on a regular basis getting IV therapy and injections in my stomach. They sent me home with injections that cost $75,000.00 that, thankfully, were covered by insurance so I did not have to pay anything. During all of this, my husband Gerald Saulsberry never left my side, never questioned me about who, what, when, how or where. God, Gerald, my children, and other family members were and still are my strength during this horrific process. I had to apologize to my husband for not confiding in him first, but I truly acted out of fear and emotion.

After the injections and other meds, I began to come back around. I was referred to Dr. Imad Omer in January but he couldn't treat the HIV/AIDS until all the other infections were cleared up. He really worked a miracle for me after six months of hospitalization to get my system cleared of all other infections I was able to start an anti-viral regimen. At the onset of my diagnosis in January 2011 I had AIDS. By July of the same year, I was downgraded to HIV which was undetectable and has been since that day.

In August, 2011 my husband was tested and his result was negative. Thank you, Jesus! As I look back over the years before I was diagnosed, I'm grateful for how things turned out. I was sick most of the time and we weren't as sexually active as newlyweds. I must admit I was mad at myself and to be honest I was mad at God. I didn't understand how God could bless me with such a wonderful man and I wasn't able to perform my wifely duties. It was at that point I knew God has blessed me with a true man who loves me unconditionally. God and my husband reminded me of our vows: in sickness and in health, till death us do part… I didn't understand then but I now know that God was saving my husband from contracting the virus I didn't even know I had.

God knows what we need even when we don't. I thank Him for allowing Gerald and I to be married every day of my life. Nothing and no one can tear us apart. Even on our worst days there is no place I'd rather be than with Gerald Saulsberry. In my lowest days Gerald was my strength. When I wanted to give up and stop taking my medicine, he was my cheerleader, encourager, fighter and friend. He never let me wallow in self defeat or pity. There were days I questioned God, wondering why me. His reply, "Why not you?" Some nights and days I would cry out in defeat.

One day the Lord answered, ***"This has nothing to do with you. You are strong and you can handle this. This illness is not unto death."***

He also said this is for someone out there that needs to know GOD CAN DO ANYTHING. He chose me for this, knowing I would give Him all the glory.

We live by faith and not by sight -1 Corinthians 5:7

I've spent a lot of my days and nights dealing with personal feelings, thoughts, and struggles to understand how God could use what I've endured and what I am going through to help someone. It's sad to say, but "saved" people were my greatest challenge. In my own struggle to believe that God would manifest healing in my body, I had believers look at me strange and question me. They acted as if I was speaking a foreign language. I could not answer their unbelief. My faith faltered and I felt guilty about my situation. I'm grateful that I was taught about God's will and His word and what it could manifest. I had to surround myself with and communicate with others that also believed in healing and miracles.

I had to disconnect from negative people. I couldn't afford to lose my belief in healing because of others' unbelief. That's why I prayed and asked God to direct me to people and who to share my status with that would earnestly pray and believe God for complete healing and wholeness with me. I've come to accept and believe our ways and thoughts are not like His ways and thoughts. He knows what's best for me. He is the Great Physician. He knows my past, my present and my future, like the woman with the issue of blood (one of my favorite stories in the Bible). In Luke the woman with the issue of blood bled for twelve long years. She had gone to every doctor and spent all she had trying to stop the flow. She was considered unclean and was told she could not be among people, but she heard Jesus was coming through. He was on his way to see about Jarius's daughter. She heard this and disobeyed the law of the land and pressed her way through the crowd to get to Jesus. She said if she could just touch the hem of his garment she would be healed. She made her way through the crowd and touched Jesus's hem. Jesus asked who had touched him. His disciples responded, noting the crowd, wondering why would Jesus ask such a question: "All these people and you ask *who touched you?*"

He said it was a different touch because the virtue had left him. The lady came forth admitting it was her and Jesus looked at her and said, "Daughter your faith has healed you. Go in peace." (Luke 8:48).

Reflections

Do you believe in healing and miracles? Why or why not?

____

____

____

Connecting with positive people is a must when believing God for something. How do you handle negative people and negative situations?

____

____

____

If faced with a diagnosis of a terminal illness, how do you think you would handle it?

____

____

____

Snap out of depression, your attitude determines your altitude!

Another Storm

This is the confidence we have in approaching God—that if we ask anything according to His will he hears us—whatever we ask—we know that we have what we asked of Him.
1 John 5:14-15

On December 5, 2011 I went into St. Francis Hospital to have a total thyroidectomy. I was diagnosed with hypothyroidism in 1985 with a goiter the size of a dime then. By 2011 the goiter had grown to the size of a large lemon and it was so big it that it was pushing down and shifting my heart. It was hard to breathe and harder to lie down. It had gotten to the point that I had to sleep on two pillows and sometimes I even had to sleep sitting up. I went into surgery and immediately after, I was put in ICU for a day then moved to a regular room. The next night I was struggling to breathe, so they called a specialist to do a test to find out why. It turns out both my vocal chords had been damaged and weren't working. They took me back to surgery on December 7th to put a tracheotomy in to help with my breathing.

After surgery they realized I was not able to talk at all because my vocal chords had completely shut down. I thought I would be able to talk after they put the trach in but I could not. I could not utter a sound. The trach was only to help me breathe. The doctors were trying to keep from putting me on the ventilator. What was supposed to be an outpatient procedure turned out to be a two-week ordeal. I had to be hospitalized that long because they had to train my family members how to take care of and clean the trach. My daughter Jamillia was the only one that could stand it and wanted to be trained because the others were nervous.

While in the hospital I did not complain one time. Was I scared? Absolutely! I went from talking to not being able to talk or breathe without a trach in a matter of two days. I got out of the hospital a week before Christmas and that was a trying time. I went home not able to talk and had to communicate via text message or writing pad. Things I took for granted were lost in the blink of an eye. I couldn't blow on my food to cool it down when it was hot. I could not drink liquids, even water. I had to eat ice cubes and popsicles for seven months for fear of choking. My breathing was coming out of my neck through the trach. My husband, mother, sister and children took very good care of me during my down time. I also had to sleep sitting up in a recliner for the first four months. Through it all I never doubted God would give me my voice back.

In March 2012, after being out sick for three months the doctor released me to return to work, but I was terrified to go back. I was embarrassed about the trach in my neck. I had been in the house for the entire time, only going out to my doctor appointments. I didn't even go to church. The first day back I sat in my car and cried. My husband had to talk me into going in. I still wasn't talking so I performed tasked that didn't require me being on the phone like filing and processing paperwork. I am eternally grateful for my job at Trumbull Lab because they made provisions for me to work. They could have easily sent me home. Everyone was so receptive and made me feel comfortable, but still there were days I didn't think I was going to make it. Not only was I dealing with the trach, but also with my HIV/AIDS diagnosis.

The healing process was long and hard. I had to go to the Ear Nose Throat Specialist every two weeks to see if my vocal cords were working, so the trach could be removed. Appointment after appointment there was no change. I was not completely satisfied with the ENT doctor I was going to so I sought a second opinion. One of the doctors in the lab I worked in referred me to Dr. Neal Beckford, ENT. I started going to see him every week and after four months, in July 2012 the trach was removed and my breathing was fine.

When my voice came back, Dr. Beckford expected it to be hoarse and weak, but it was as strong as ever. Prior to the surgery I was in the choir and I thought I would never be able to sing again. But against all odds I got back in the choir and led a song. Praise and glory unto God, I've been talking ever since with no problem. However, my left vocal cord is completely damaged and I only have one functioning vocal cord, but you can't tell. I am truly a walking, breathing miracle. And God left me a reminder: the scar where the trach used to be; just like Jesus was identified after he hung on the cross: BY HIS SCARS!

Reflections

Have you ever gone through a situation one way and it turned out another way? How did you handle the change in the situation?

____

____

____

You know in life we take things for granted, simple things such as blowing your food cool or being able to talk. If those things were taken from you, how would you handle it?

____

____

____

What gets you through your toughest times?

____

____

____

Hold on to your healing!

Nahum 1:7, 9b

Lessons Learned

After many hospital stays because of HIV and thyroid surgery and countless other things here are some things I've learned:

I know nothing will ever be this hard again. I know there was a purpose in going through all this. I always say: the thing about teaching someone a lesson through trials is you have no control over how they'll eventually use it.

***

I've decided to take life one day at a time. I realized there are people who love me and that I love very much. If they are willing to accept me just the way I am, and are willing to go on this journey with me, who am I to quit?

***

Even though scientists have no hope for curing HIV/AIDS, I still believe with everything in me I will be healed completely like the woman with the issue of blood and the man with leprosy. My faith will make me WHOLE. After years of expensive medicine, this disease will completely reverse itself.

***

I will always be grateful, not just for my health, but for those individuals who sacrificed and prayed for me. I resist temptation every day to look back and complain. Instead, I concentrate on what God promised me. I may have ninety-nine problems but my faith is not one!

Everyday Meditation Instructions!

1. Believe the scriptures every time you read them. *Confess with your mouth.*

2. Believe them on purpose. (Make them final authority in your life).

3. Believe: this is Jesus speaking to me

4. Use "in Jesus's Name" after every scripture. That seals it.

5. Say "I BELIEVE IT."

6. Feed the scriptures into your spirit.

7. From time to time remind God what He said in His word!!!!

Healing Scriptures from *King James Version*

Meditate on these scriptures (DAILY)

Exodus 15:26

I am the Lord that health thee.

Exodus 23:25-26

And ye shall serve the Lord your God, and He shall bless thy bread, and thy water: and I will take sickness away from the midst of thee. There shall nothing cast their young, nor be barren in thy land: the number of thy days I will fulfill.

Deuteronomy 7:15

The Lord will keep you free from every disease. He will not inflict on you the horrible diseases you knew in Egypt, but he will inflict them on all who hate you.

Psalm 30:2

O Lord my God, I cried unto thee, and thou has healed me.

Psalm 91:10

There shall no evil befall thee, neither shall any plague come nigh thy dwelling.

Psalm 103:2-5

Bless the Lord, O my soul, and forget not all his benefits: Who forgiveth all thine iniquities; who healeth all thy diseases; Who redeemeth thy life from destruction; who crowneth thee with loving kindness and tender mercies; Who satisfieth thy mouth with good things; so that thy youth is renewed like the eagle's.

Psalm 107:20

He sent his word, and healeth them, and delivered them from their destructions.

Proverbs 3:7-8

Be not wise in thine own eyes: fear the Lord, and depart from evil. It shall be health to thy navel, and marrow to thy bones.

Isaiah 53:4-5

Surely he hath borne our griefs, and carried our sorrows: yet we did esteem him stricken, smitten of God, and afflicted. But he was wounded for our transgressions, he was bruised for our iniquities: the chastisement of our peace was upon him; and with his stripes we are healed.

Jeremiah 30:17

For I will restore health unto thee, and I will heal thy wounds, saith the Lord;

Malachi 4:2

But unto you that fear my name shall the Sun of righteousness arise with healing in his wings; and ye shall go forth, and grow up as calves of the stall.

Matthew 8:17

That it might be fulfilled which was spoken by Esaias the prophet, saying, Himself took our infirmities, and bare our sicknesses.

Matthew 14:14

And Jesus went forth, and saw a great multitude, and was moved with compassion toward them, and he healed their sick,

Mark 1:40-42

And there came to a leper to him, beseeching him, and kneeling down to him, and saying unto him, if though canst make me clean. And Jesus, moved with compassion, put forth his hand, and touched him, and saith unto him, I will; be thou clean. And as soon as he had spoken, immediately the leprosy departed from him, and he was cleansed.

1 Peter 2:24

Who his own self bare our sins in his own body on the tree, that we, being dead to sin, should live unto righteousness: by whose stripes ye were healed.

3 John 2

Beloved, I wish above all things that thou mayest prosper and be in health, even as thy soul prospereth.

Mark 16:17-18

And these signs shall follow them that believe: In my name…they shall lay hands on the sick, and they shall recover.

SIDENOTE: Find someone who believes God's word regarding healing and have them lay hands on you and pray for you in faith, believing James 5:16 that says, "the effectual fervent prayer of a righteous man avails much."

Isaiah 40:31

But they that wait upon the Lord shall renew their strength; they shall mount up with wings as eagles; they shall run, and not be weary, and shall walk and not faint,

SIDENOTE: The word "wait" implies a positive action of hope based on knowing that the Word of God is a true fact and that it will soon come to pass—WAIT WITH EARNEST EXPECTATION!

Psalm 34:19

Many are the afflictions of the righteous, but the Lord delivers him out of them all.

Isaiah 53:4-5

Surely He hath borne our griefs [sickness] and carried our sorrows [pains] yet we did esteem Him stricken, smitten of God and afflicted, but He was wounded for our transgressions, He was bruised for our iniquities; the chastisement of our peace was upon Him; by His stripes we are Healed.

SIDENOTE: The last part of this verse (healed) is not talking about spiritual healing, as some have taught, but definite physical healing. God does not "heal" a human spirit, He recreates it. He does, however, heal our bodies and minds. This clearly shows that our healing was paid for on the cross!

Jeremiah 33:6

Behold, I will bring you heath and cure, and I will cure you, and will reveal unto you the abundance of peace and truth."

Matthew 18:19

Again I say to you that if two of you agree on earth concerning anything that they ask, it will be done for them by my father in Heaven,

SIDENOTE: The prayer of agreement is powerful—partner with someone to agree with you for your healing!

Mark 11:24

Therefore I say to you whatever things you ask when you pray, believe that you receive them, and you will have them.

SIDENOTE: Absolutely! This includes healing!

Isaiah 58:8

Thy light shall break forth as the morning, and thy health shall spring forth speedily; and thy righteousness shall go before thee: the glory of the Lord shall be they rear guard.

1 Thessalonians 5:23

And the very God of peace sanctify you wholly; and I pray God your whole spirit and soul and body be preserved blameless unto the coming of our Lord Jesus Christ.

SIDENOTE: It is very clear in this passage that wholeness, wellness, and health are for the complete make-up of man: spiritual, mental and physical.

1 Peter 2:24

Who himself bore our sins in His own body on the tree, that we having died to sins, might live for righteousness---by whose stripes you are healed.

SIDENOTE: Past tense, "you *were* healed." Jesus paid it all for your total deliverance, spirit, soul and body!

Psalm 103:2-3

Bless the Lord. O my soul, and forget not all his benefits: Who forgiveth all thine iniquities, who heals all thy diseases.

SIDENOTE: It doesn't say "SOME," it says "ALL!" It also states that healing is one of the benefits that belongs to the believer along with the benefit of having our sins forgiven.

3 John 2

Beloved, I wish above all things that thou mayest prosper and be in health, even as thy soul prospereth.

Jeremiah 17:14

Heal me. O Lord, and I shall be healed, save me, and I shall be saved; for thou art my praise.

SIDENOTE: Once you finally sees that healing is a finished work along with salvation, paid for at the same time with the same healing blood, then you can get excited about the verse saying, "YOU DID IT LORD FOR ME." Then according to this verse agree and say, "I will have healing just as I have salvation, IT'S TIME NOW!"

James 5:14

Is any sick among you? Let him call for the elders of the church, and let them pray over him, anointing him with oil in the name of the Lord: And the prayer of faith shall save the sick, and the Lord shall raise him up; and if he have committed sins, they shall be forgiven him.

Psalm 30:2

O Lord my God, I cried unto thee, and thou has healed me.

Psalm 119:50

This is my comfort in my affliction, for your word has given my life.

Romans 10:17

So then faith comes by hearing and hearing by the word of God.

SIDENOTE: Faith for healing comes by hearing God's word concerning healing. Just as you may be taking medicine two or three times a day, do the same thing with the promises in the word of God regarding healing and allow your faith to be built up! You will be amazed at the change that will take place.

Proverbs 4:20-22

My Son, attend to my words; incline thine ear unto my sayings. Let them not depart from thine eyes; keep them in the midst of thine heart. For they are life unto those that find them, and health (medicine) to all their flesh.

SIDENOTE: In this verse it is as plain as can be: taking God's word is life and medicine to your flesh. So just take your prescribed natural medicine and add the word of God along with it. Prescribed medicine can heal and help some things, but God's medicine can heal all.

Isaiah 55:11

So shall my word be that goeth forth out of my mouth: it shall not return unto me void, but it shall accomplish that which I please, and it shall prosper in the thing whereto I sent it.

SIDENOTE: God's word on healing will accomplish healing in you.

Snap Out of That Depression, Your Attitude Determines Your Altitude!

Hebrews 12:12-13

Wherefore lift up the hands which hang down, and the feeble knees; and make straight paths for your feet, lest that which is lame be turned out of the way; but let it rather be healed."

SIDENOTE: Real faith rejoices at the promises of God as if it were experiencing them already. Get the focus off of your problem and on the answer, which are the promises of GOD—His Word. REJOICE. GET HAPPY. IT'S ALL YOURS!!!!

Hebrews 10:23

Let us hold fast the profession of our faith without wavering; (for he is faithful that promised).

SIDENOTE: Remember Hebrews 6: 18 says that it's impossible for God to lie!

1 John 5:14-15

Now this is the confidence that we have in Him, that if we ask anything according to His will, He hear us. And if we know He hear us, whatever we ask, we know that we have the petitions that we ask of Him.

SIDENOTE: It's easy to know the will of God. The Word of God is the will of God! Jeremiah 1:12 says, "He watches over His Word to perform it." So when you ask and believe the Word of God you are asking and believing according to His will and you will receive, just as it says!

Hebrews 10: 35-36

Therefore do not cast away your confidence, which has great reward. For you have need of endurance, so that after you have done the will of God, you may receive the promise.

SIDENOTE: Remember the Will of God is the Word of God!

Your Words Are Important!

Mark 11:22-23

And Jesus answering saith unto them, Have faith in God. For verily I say unto you, that whosoever shall say unto this mountain, be thou removed, and be thou cast into the sea; and shall not doubt in his heart, but shall believe that those things which he saith shall come to pass; he shall have whatsoever he saith.

SIDENOTE: What kind of mountains or obstacles do you have in your life right now? Obey Jesus and command that mountain of pain, cancer, HIV/AIDS, any form of disease, to go NOW out of your body in the name of Jesus. Jesus said you can have whatever you say. Begin to call your body whole, healed, and well—don't stop, don't listen to your body, don't listen to doubt and fear, listen to Jesus, and study His Word!

Remember To Give Testimony Of Your Healing!

Revelation 12:11

And they overcame him by the blood of the Lamb, and by the Word of their testimony…

SIDENOTE: When your healing manifests itself and you recover and have the opportunity to testify to the grace of the Lord—DO IT! The Lord wants you to give glory to Him for what he has done and it will also serve to help build faith in someone else who has a need.

Hold On To Your Healing!

Nahum 1:7, 9b

The Lord is good, a stronghold in the day of trouble; and He knows those who trust in Him…. He will make an utter end of it. Affliction will not rise up a second time."

SIDENOTE: After you've received the manifestation of healing, this becomes your stand of FAITH!